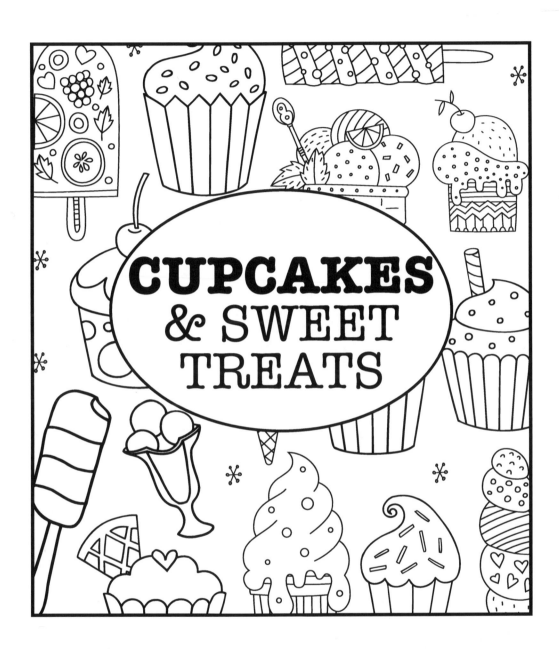

CUPCAKES & SWEET TREATS

Gorgeous Colouring For Girls Book 9

First published in 2016 by Kyle Craig Publishing

Text and illustration copyright © 2016 Kyle Craig Publishing

Editor: Alison McNicol

Design: Elizabeth James, Julie Anson, Alison McNicol, Shutterstock, Inc.

ISBN: 978-1-78595-162-6

A CIP record for this book is available from the British Library.

A Kyle Craig Publication

www.kyle-craig.com

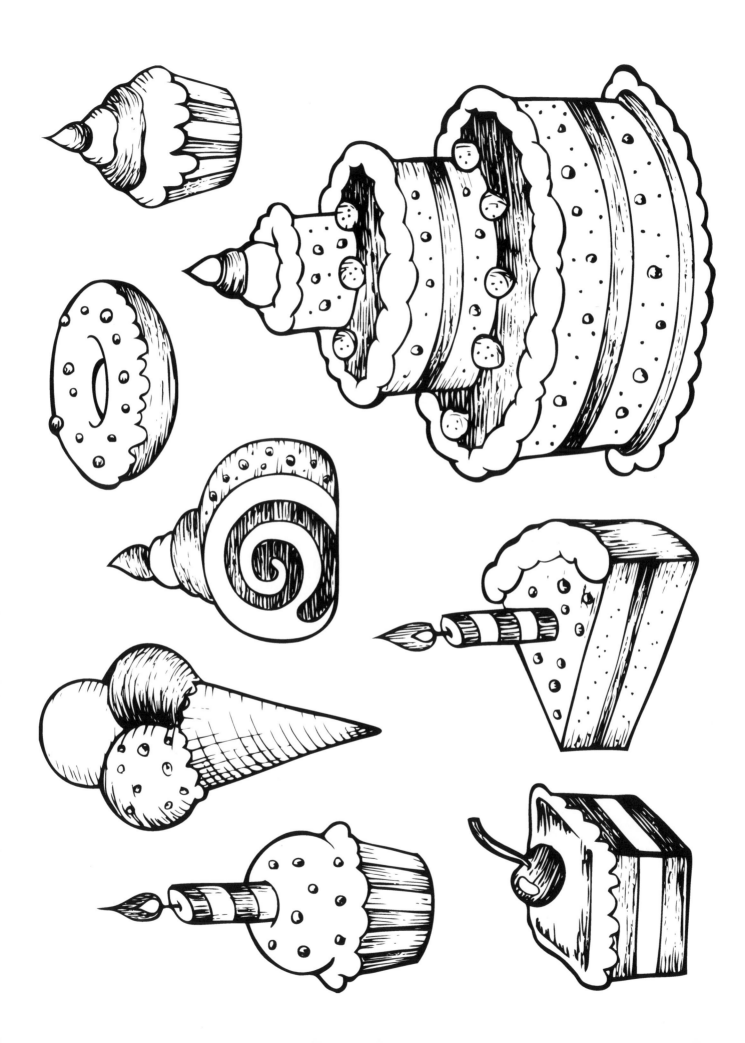

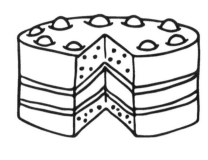
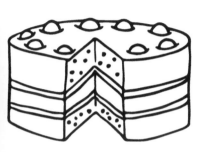

Tea
Party

Printed in Great Britain
by Amazon